LE BOURGEOIS GENTILHOMME

Molière

LE BOURGEOIS GENTILHOMME

A new version by Nick Dear

OBERON BOOKS
LONDON

WWW.OBERONBOOKS.COM

First published in 1992 by Oberon Books Ltd
521 Caledonian Road, London N7 9RH
Tel: +44 (0) 20 7607 3637 / Fax: +44 (0) 20 7607 3629
e-mail: info@oberonbooks.com
www.oberonbooks.com

A catalogue record for this book is available from the British Library.

ISBN: 978-0-94823-053-0

Printed and bound by Marston Book Services Ltd, Didcot.

Visit www.oberonbooks.com to read more about all our books
and to buy them. You will also find features, author interviews and
news of any author events, and you can sign up for e-newsletters
so that you're always first to hear about our new releases.

Characters

M. JOURDAIN	(A bourgeois)
MME. JOURDAIN	(His wife)
LUCILE	(His daughter)
NICOLE	(Their maid)
CLÉONTE	(In love with Lucile)
COVIELLE	(Cléonte's valet)
DORANTE	(A Count)
DORIMÈNE	(A Countess)
MUSIC MASTER	
DANCING MASTER	
FENCING INSTRUCTOR	
PROFESSOR OF PHILOSOPHY	
TAILOR	
TWO VALETS	
THE MUFTI	

SINGERS, DANCERS, MUSICIANS, COOKS, APPRENTICES

Introduction

I suspect that Molière wrote this very fast, intuitively, without research. It has that kind of feel. In 1670 Louis the Fourteenth commissioned a musical entertainment from his court composer, Lully. At a late stage Molière was requested to provide, please, some amusing scenes of drama. (Playwrights get used to this sort of thing.) The initial description of the piece was 'a comedy ballet'. We must remember that the dances which punctuate the play, and the musical interludes, were of equal status with the dramatic action. And that the show originally ended with a huge *'Ballet des Nations'* – the kind of court spectacular typical for the period – which may account for the slight sense of anti-climax one feels on concluding the written text today. In performance the final revels should be as grand as resources allow. We mustn't let our imaginations be too fettered by mere words.

The key to understanding the enduring value of his plays lies, I think, in the exquisite intuition of its author. The plotting is rough, the humour sometimes silly, yet Monsieur Jourdain remains fresh. Molière was writing a century before what we have come to call 'the middle class' wrestled power, in France, from a decadent, feudal monarchy. He had his finger on a social pulse that would grow into the irresistible marching beat of *sans-culottes* drums. He anatomises a man who is at the same time a figure of fun and an instrument of power. He catches Jourdain, the bourgeois, on the cusp of historical predominance – at a time when he could be laughed at and laughed with, but not yet feared. Molière is both so much in touch with his own time, and so far in advance of it, that he instinctively knows this character is truly important, but he isn't quite certain *why*. Because of this, the resolution of the story is ambivalent: Jourdain is judged and found to be a fool, sure, but he isn't *damned*. In the end, he remains in command.

Traditionally, the English theatre likes to laugh at Jourdain and not with him. Apart from the rare outbreaks of unruliness, we have always clutched at the comfy cushion of the status quo. But is this the manner in which this play is actually written? Jourdain is, of course, satirised. He is shown to be foolish, proud, bossy and ignorant. What redeems him, however, is his passionate longing for knowledge. In some respects (not all), he's aware of his limitations. "I'm stupid. Teach me!" is the constant refrain of the first half of the play. This should generate sympathy. Only in the mind of the snob does it invite contempt. But then the English theatre has long been safe haven for the snob, as no doubt was the Sun King's theatre at Versailles.

In fact, Moilère's most vicious satire is directed at the establishment figures: composer, tailor, philosopher and so on. These are the people who are really stupid, because these are the people who have lost all desire to improve themselves. These are the ones who are convinced their system is *right*. They think they are the ultimate, and thus they have come to a halt. Surpassing them on wretchedness are the gentry, whose lives are filled with nothing more substantial than the quest for sensual pleasure. Jourdain of course yearns to join them in this; he's no saint. But whereas he has the means – that is, the wealth – to pursue these ambitions, he nonetheless remains extremely naive and gullible. Everyone makes a fool of him, despite the fact that he's the most powerful person on stage. It's as if he hasn't yet learnt how to marshal his bourgeoning power; in a sense he is not ready for it. He's like a man who sits down at a piano for the very first time. Today, all he can make is a terrible noise. Tomorrow, he'll play a sonata.

Am I judging the play with the benefit of hindsight? Of course. How else can you judge a play? This piece has survived three centuries – three centuries! – because its internal dynamic is much richer and more provocative than a quick reading of its light comedy might seem to admit. Molière's dramatic nose led him, once again, to buried truffles. . .proving, once again, that it's not necessary to write 'political' stories in order to pick the threads of society apart.

Nick Dear

Le Bourgeois Gentilhomme received its British première in this version at the National Theatre in April 1992. The cast was as follows:

M. JOURDAIN	Timothy Spall
MME. JOURDAIN	Anita Dobson
LUCILE	Cathryn Bradshaw
NICOLE	Janine Duvitski
CLÉONTE	Adam Kotz
COVIELLE	Teddy Kempner
DORANTE	Duncan Bell
DORIMÈNE	Cecily Hobbs
MUSIC MASTER	Steven Beard
DANCING MASTER	Mark Hadfield
FENCING INSTRUCTOR	Paul M. Meston
PROFESSOR OF PHILOSOPHY	Myra McFadyen
TAILOR	Brian Lipson
VALET	Charles Simon
VALET	John Boswall
TAILOR APPRENTICE	Adrian Schiller
MUSIC STUDENTS, DANCING STUDENTS, TAILORS, COOKS	Ian Caddick, John Cobb, Sonya Leite, Nick Mercer, Gerald Salih

Director	Richard Jones
Set Design	The Brothers Quay
Costumes	Nicky Gillibrand
Lighting	Scott Zielinski
Music	Jonathan Dove/ Jean Baptiste-Lulli
Company Voice Work	Patsy Rodenburg
Choreographer	Michael Popper
Musical Director	Eleanor Alberga

ACT ONE

Paris, 1670. The house of M. Jourdain. Inside the house, the MUSIC STUDENT works on hot composition. Enter from outside the MUSIC MASTER and the DANCING MASTER, with their MUSICIANS and DANCERS.

MUSIC MASTER: Come along in, and wait over there.

DANCING MASTER: Dancers, wait this side.

MUSIC MASTER: *(To the MUSIC STUDENT.)* Finished yet? *(The MUSIC STUDENT hands him a manuscript.)*

MUSIC MASTER: *(READING.)* This is very good.

DANCING MASTER: Have you something new?

MUSIC MASTER: I have provided the inspiration for my pupil to compose an original serenade, whilst our friend is getting up.

DANCING MASTER: Can I see it?

MUSIC MASTER: No you can't. You shall hear it when our friend deigns to put in appearance. It won't take him much longer to dress. I hope.

DANCING MASTER: We are kept extremely busy you and I.

MUSIC MASTER: We are.

DANCING MASTER: A long, hard round of perpetual creativity.

MUSIC MASTER: Because we've just found the man we both needed. What could be more fruitful, than to be in the employ of a simple person who has allowed the seed of high and gracious living to take root in his brain? If there were more like Monsieur Jourdain is society, music and the dance would be far better off.

DANCING MASTER: I agree. Up to a point. But I'd be happier if he had a marginally more sophisticated understanding of the gifts we offer him.

MUSIC MASTER: He's not exactly a connoisseur. But he pays well. And in the modern world, serious art needs sponsorship if it is to survive.

DANCING MASTER: Of course, but I confess that nothing spurs me on to yet higher achievement that the occasional bask in glory. I have a wee penchant for sustained applause. It is torture for the artist to have to perform to idiots, and then to have to listen to their witless, vulgar chat. Pleasure derives, if I may just finish, in the refined audience, who appreciate the subtler points of one's creations, and who reward one's tireless labour with their praise and high esteem.

MUSIC MASTER: But you can't eat good reviews. The surest way of showing enjoyment is writing your name on a cheque. And this is where our friend excels. As for his critical faculties, well, plainly, the lights are on but there's nobody home. He talks the most incredible drivel about every subject known to man, but his gold makes up for his ghastly taste. He is a connoisseur of the bankroll.

DANCING MASTER: I concur. Partially. Yet surely this preoccupation with money is beneath such maestro as yourself?

MUSIC MASTER: I have never seen you shun the proffered purse, maestro.

DANCING MASTER: No, no, but I take it with a heavy heart, maestro, for I dearly wish his beneficence were seasoned with good taste.

MUSIC MASTER: I wish so too. But if nothing else, we're in work. Think of your reputation. All Paris will adore us, and our friend will foot the bill. *(Enter M. JOURDAIN with two VALETS.)*

M. JOURDAIN: Right, are we set for the knees-up?

DANCING MASTER: Excuse me?

M. JOURDAIN: The sing-song?

MUSIC MASTER: Sing-song?

M. JOURDAIN: What do you call it, then? Spot of singing, spot of dancing, all on the go at once? You know: the show.

DANCING MASTER: Ah, the show.

MUSIC MASTER: We are holding ourselves in readiness.

M. JOURDAIN: Yea, I'm sorry to keep you waiting, but today I want to be done up nice and smart, you see, and my bloody tailor sent me a pair of silk stockings so tight I thought they'd never get over my knees. Neither of you are to leave the premises until they deliver my new suit. I want you to see me turned out from top to tail like a real gentleman. It's the very latest style, I do assure you.

MUSIC MASTER: We have no doubt of that.

M. JOURDAIN: Meanwhile I had this oriental number run up just for me. *(His dressing gown.)*

DANCING MASTER: How divine.

M. JOURDAIN: My tailor informs me that all the class people adopt one of these before lunch. Valet!

VALET 1: Can I get you something, sir?

M. JOURDAIN: No, just making sure that you've washed out your ears. – Marvellous people, servants. What do you think of their livery?

DANCING MASTER: Exquisite. *(M. JOURDAIN opens his robe to reveal red breeches and a green jacket.)*

MUSIC MASTER: Very dashing.

M. JOURDAIN: Valet!

VALET 1: Sir?

M. JOURDAIN: No, not you, the other one. What's the point of having two if the sod does all the work?

VALET 2: Sir?

M JOURDAIN: Hold my dressing gown. – Do I still look the business?

DANCING MASTER: Incomparable.

M. JOURDAIN: Then let's get on with your prologue or epigraph or whatever it is.

MUSIC MASTER: Prior to that I should like you to hear the serenade which you commissioned. I set one of my most talented students to it.

M. JOURDAIN: A student? You gave the job to a bone-idle student? What's wrong with doing it yourself?

MUSIC MASTER: It is normally considered a great honour to have music composed for you by a student of mine.

M. JOURDAIN: Oh? Well that's all right then. Off you go. *(The SINGER begins.)* – Give us my gown back so I can listen properly. – No, wait, I think I'll be better without it. – On second thoughts I will wear it after all.

SINGER: *(Song.)* My heart burns with a fire that is ceaselessly roaring:

One look into your eyes, and my wits are derang'd.

If you treat thus a man, cruel love, so adoring –

Alas! what distress comes to he, who from you is estrang'd?

M. JOURDAIN: *(Yawn.)* What a bloody dreary song. No chance of jollying it up, I suppose?

MUSIC MASTER: Monsieur, the air must suit the mood of the words.

M. JOURDAIN: I feared as much. I knew a song once. Very witty it was too. How did it go again?

DANCING MASTER: Good God, how do I know?

M. JOURDAIN: Had a girl in it. And a sheep.

DANCING MASTER: A girl and a sheep?

M. JOURDAIN: Yes. It's coming back to me now. . . *(Sings.)*
Oh, Janet, Janet, Janet, Janet, Janet,
Every time I talk of love you try to ban it;
I thought your heart you'd open to me deep,
But I find that you're a wolf dressed as a sheep.
Oh Janet;
Dear Janet;

> When I see your woolly tail it makes me weep.
> – Don't you think that's beautiful?

MUSIC MASTER: Very beautiful indeed.

DANCING MASTER: And you sing it beautifully.

M. JOURDAIN: Though I never studied music. Incredible.

MUSIC MASTER: You should study music, Monsieur, as you study the dance. They go together as a matter of fact.

M. JOURDAIN: Do proper people study music? I mean – lords and ladies?

MUSIC MASTER: Yes they do.

M. JOURDAIN: Right, then so will I. But I don't know when I'm going to fit it into my schedule. As well as the Fencing Instructor who's giving me lessons, I've a Philosophy chap due to start this morning.

MUSIC MASTER: Philosophy's not bad, but music –

DANCING MASTER: Dance, music and dance, are the absolute necessities of life –

MUSIC MASTER: The State needs music.

DANCING MASTER: People need to dance.

MUSIC MASTER: All the war, all the chaos in the world stems from lack of the study of music.

DANCING MASTER: All the misery of mankind, all the downfall of history, all the stupidity of politicians, all the blunders of generals, in short, everything, comes from never having learned how to dance.

M. JOURDAIN: You're going to have to explain this in a little more detail.

MUSIC MASTER: Tell me what war is, if not a discord between two nations?

M. JOURDAIN: You're right.

MUSIC MASTER: Well, if every citizen of every nation studied music, wouldn't they have a better appreciation of the potential for harmony in the world?

M. JOURDAIN: You are right!

DANCING MASTER: And don't we always say, when a man has made a serious error in public or private life, don't we always say "He stepped out of line"?

M. JOURDAIN: We do, don't we.

DANCING MASTER: And why did he step out of line? Because he did not know how to dance!

M. JOURDAIN: Both of you are quite right.

MUSIC MASTER: Then would you like to see our performance now?

M. JOURDAIN: Yes please.

MUSIC MASTER: The first piece is an exercise in the portrayal of the passions, musically. *(To SINGERS.)* Would you mind, please? – You must envisage them dressed as shepherds.

M. JOURDAIN: Not shepherds again. It's always bleeding shepherds. Can't I have water-nymphs?

MUSIC MASTER: No. It is called the pastoral convention. They are expressing their innermost passions in song. Would it seem natural to have water-nymphs expressing their innermost passions in song? It would not.

It must be shepherds. Who are like that.
(He claps his hands and the music begins.)

Duet.

MAN:
We lie in love's garden
For long, golden hours;
Two hearts young and ardent,
Two exquisite flowers.

WOMAN:
This heat does delight now,
But summer wanes;
I feel winter's cold snow
Course through my veins.

BOTH:
Serenade life!
Serenade love!
Sing for peace and tranquillity –
Nothing on earth lasts for eternity.

M. JOURDAIN:
Is that all?

MUSIC MASTER:
Yes.

M. JOURDAIN:
Strikingly, resoundingly brilliant. As far as I can tell.

DANCING MASTER:
And now, for my offering, I humbly present the most beautiful movements available to the human body.

M. JOURDAIN:
Shepherds again?

DANCING MASTER:
Whatever you like, Monsieur. – Begin!
(Music. A dance.)

M. JOURDAIN:
That wasn't quite as pathetic as I expected. Some of those shepherds can wiggle very nicely.

MUSIC MASTER:
When the dancing's put together with the music, the whole effect will be considerably improved.

M. JOURDAIN: Good. It's intended for a very special lady who is doing me the honour of dropping in for a bite to eat.

DANCING MASTER: Everything's ready.

MUSIC MASTER: Except a detail which Monsieur has apparently overlooked.

M. JOURDAIN: Oh? What?

MUSIC MASTER: A gentleman, Monsieur, of such taste and discernment as yourself, would normally at this point in the season have arranged for a recital in his salon every Wednesday, say, or Thursday.

M. JOURDAIN: That's what the posh do, is it?

MUSIC MASTER: Yes, Monsieur.

M. JOURDAIN: See to it then. Make sure there's plenty of noise.

MUSIC MASTER: Oh, there will be! So long as you hire three singers – soprano, counter-tenor, and bass – accompanied by viol da gamba, lute and harpsichord for the basso continuo, and two violins for the ritornello.

M. JOURDAIN: I shall also require a bagpipe. The bagpipe is my favourite instrument and will sound extremely harmonious with those other things. But the crucial task for today is that you get the entertainment bang-on at dinner time.

DANCING MASTER: I am sure you will be delighted with it. The minuet especially is, forgive me for saying so, a triumph.

M. JOURDAIN: Oh, a minuet? The minuet is my dance! You must see how I've improved! Maestro, please . . .

DANCING MASTER: Sir, you cannot dance without a hat.

M. JOURDAIN: I can't?

MUSIC MASTER: Of course not. *(M. JOURDAIN puts on a hat and dances with the DANCING MASTER.)*

DANCING MASTER: La, la, la, la… *(Etc.)* …to the beat, Monsieur, to the beat…right leg, shoulders…arms…left leg…head…chin …point your toes! point your toes!

M. JOURDAIN: I'm trying!

MUSIC MASTER: Bravo!

M. JOURDAIN: Phew! That's enough. What I want to know is this. What's the protocol when a countess walks into the room? Am I meant to bow or what?

DANCING MASTER: A countess?

M. JOURDAIN: A real countess, whose name is Dorimène.

DANCING MASTER: And you wish to show respect?

M. JOURDAIN: The utmost respect.

DANCING MASTER: For the utmost respect, take a step back, and bow, than three steps forwards, bowing each time as you advance towards her, so that at the culmination of the final bow your nose is on a level with her knees. *(DANCING MASTER demonstrates. M. JOURDAIN follows.)*

M. JOURDAIN: Nose on a level with her knees. . .things are looking up already…

VALET: Monsieur, the Fencing Instructor has arrived. *(Enter FENCING INSTRUCTOR. A foil is given to M. JOURDAIN.)*

FENCING INSTRUCTOR:

Monsieur! Your salute! – Now stand up straight. Displace the centre of gravity on to the left thigh. Wrist parallel with the hip. The point of your foil in line with your shoulder. Left hand at eye level. Chin up. Hard stare. Lunge! Hold your body firm! Engage my foil in quart, and thrust. One, two. Again! Feet steady! Advance, one, two, engage my foil in tierce, and thrust. Retire to rest position. Now me. En garde, Monsieur! En garde! *(FENCING INSTRUCTOR attacks M. JOURDAIN, scoring several hits.)*

M. JOURDAIN: Christ, take it easy!

FENCING INSTRUCTOR:

Monsieur, I have repeatedly explained to you that the essence of the ancient art of swordplay can be summed up in two things. One, you give. Two, you don't receive. Last lesson I demonstrated by a deductive logic how it is impossible for you to be hit so long as you turn your opponent's foil from the line of your body. This requires no more than a flick of the wrist: thus.

M. JOURDAIN: So, if I've got it right, by this brilliant technique a man can kill another without getting killed himself, even if he is slightly deficient in courage?

FENCING INSTRUCTOR:

Exactly. What this proves above all else is the true worth of my profession, and

the ultimate superiority of the science
of weapons over such useless pseudo-
sciences as dancing and music and –

DANCING MASTER: One moment, pugilist. I must require you
to accord the ballet due respect.

MUSIC MASTER: And be rather more civil about music,
too.

FENCING INSTRUCTOR:
You should be grateful that I mention
your professions in even the same breath
as my own, you pair of comedians.

MUSIC MASTER: You're getting above yourself, sir!

DANCING MASTER: A freak with an armour-plated gut.

FENCING INSTRUCTOR:
My dear dancing master, if I choose I will
make you dance till your dick drops off.
And my dear music master, one slash will
have you trilling higher than you ever
dreamed.

DANCING MASTER: I think, metal brain, I shall be forced to
give you a taste of your own medicine.

M. JOURDAIN: *(To DANCING MASTER.)* Are you picking
a fight with a gent who understands the
essence of tierce and quart and can kill a
man by reductive logic? You're insane!

DANCING MASTER: I piss on reductive logic. I shit on his
tierce and quart.

FENCING INSTRUCTOR:
What! Impertinent runt!

M. JOURDAIN: Gentlemen, please don't quarrel.

DANCING MASTER: You have all the grace of a cart-horse in
mud!

22

FENCING INSTRUCTOR:
If I get within striking distance –

M. JOURDAIN: Calm down, calm down!

DANCING MASTER: I'll pirouette on your face!

M. JOURDAIN: For Christ's sake, stop!

FENCING INSTRUCTOR:
I'll slice you into chops!

M. JOURDAIN: I beg you!

MUSIC MASTER: Go on, teach the twat some manners.

M. JOURDAIN: Oh, don't you start!

VALET: Monsieur, the Professor of Philosophy has arrived. *(Enter the PROFESSOR OF PHILOSOPHY.)*

M. JOURDAIN: My Professor of Philosophy! In the nick of time! Come and help me restore some peace in here.

PROFESSOR OF PHILOSOPHY:
What are the parameters of the problem, gentlemen?

M. JOURDAIN: They've worked themselves into such a frenzy trying to decide which of their skills is the finest that I'm afraid they might cripple each other.

PROFESSOR OF PHILOSOPHY:
Really? Gentlemen, is this wise? Have we all not read Seneca's essay "On Anger", which explains that nothing is more base, more shameful than wild, uncontrollable passion? It drags us down to the level of the beasts! We are human beings. Reason must guide our actions. Reason is the key.

DANCING MASTER: That's all well and good, Professor, but this shithead's been slandering the arts.

PROFESSOR OF PHILOSOPHY:
A wise man stands above insults. A wise man replies to vulgarity with tolerance and moderation.

FENCING INSTRUCTOR:
But they dare to compare their wank in a bucket to the grandeur of my vast and ancient science!

PROFESSOR OF PHILOSOPHY:
So? Do you compete with them out of pride? Do you think it matters who attains the highest rung on the obsolescent social ladder? Really! I believe the only thing that usefully tells us apart is the degree of our wisdom and virtue. Not brute strength or the swagger of the intellect. Besides which, these after-tea hobbies of which you speak barely deserve to be discussed in the same room as philosophy. It is pure arrogance to accord the title of art to your prissy poses, or to you vile shrieks and grunts – and to call your dog-like scuffling a science is just stretching the bounds of credulity.

FENCING INSTRUCTOR:
Up your arse, philosopher.

MUSIC MASTER: Yes, go away, gas-bag.

DANCING MASTER: And take your cheap pedantry with you.

PROFESSOR OF PHILOSOPHY:
Why, you worthless scum! No-one speaks to me like that! I have tenure at the University! *(The PROFESSOR throws himself at them and they fight.)*

M. JOURDAIN: Professor.

PROFESSOR OF PHILOSOPHY:
    Charlatans! Recreants!

M. JOURDAIN: Professor.

FENCING INSTRUCTOR:
    Cut his balls off!

M. JOURDAIN: Gentlemen.

PROFESSOR OF PHILOSOPHY:
    Animals!

M. JOURDAIN: Professor.

DANCING MASTER: Send him to hell!

M. JOURDAIN: Gentlemen.

PROFESSOR OF PHILOSOPHY:
    Turds!

M. JOURDAIN: Professor.

MUSIC MASTER: Go on! Bash him on the nose!

M. JOURDAIN: Gentlemen, please. *(They exit, still fighting.)* All right, knock seven shades of shit out of each other if you must, I'm not getting blood on my best dressing gown. *(The PROFESSOR returns, straightening his clothes.)*

PROFESSOR OF PHILOSOPHY:
    Shall we proceed with the lesson?

M. JOURDAIN: Oh, my poor Professor, I'm sorry you got such a kicking.

PROFESSOR OF PHILOSOPHY:
    In the great cosmic scheme of being, it is nothing. A philosopher must practice

complete toleration. Besides which I fully
intend to get my own back.

M. JOURDAIN: How?

PROFESSOR OF PHILOSOPHY:

I shall write a satire. In the style of
Juvenal. They shall be lashed with my
excoriating wit. But let us move on to
higher things. What would you like to
learn?

M. JOURDAIN: Absolutely everything I can. I've a terrific
thirst for knowledge. I'm so mad at my
bleeding parents for not making me study
harder when I was a kid.

PROFESSOR OF PHILOSOPHY:

A right and proper sentiment: "*Nam sine
doctrina vita est quasi mortis imago.*" You
have your Latin, of course.

M. JOURDAIN: Of course. But just for the hell of it,
imagine I left it somewhere.

PROFESSOR OF PHILOSOPHY:

Well, it means, "Without knowledge, life
is no more than a foretaste of death."

M. JOURDAIN: That Latin's shit-hot, isn't it?

PROFESSOR OF PHILOSOPHY:

Tell me, have you mastered the
rudimentary principles of scientific
discipline?

M. JOURDAIN: Oh sure. I can read and write.

PROFESSOR OF PHILOSOPHY:

Then where would you like to begin,
Monsieur? Do you wish to learn logic?

M. JOURDAIN: All right. What is it?

PROFESSOR OF PHILOSOPHY:
It consists primarily of the Three Laws of Pure Reason.

M. JOURDAIN: And what are the Three Laws of Pure Reason?

PROFESSOR OF PHILOSOPHY:
Well, there's the First Law of Pure Reason, the Second Law of Pure Reason, and the Third Law of Pure Reason.

M. JOURDAIN: I'm with you so far.

PROFESSOR OF PHILOSOPHY:
The First Law appertaining to the operation of the human mind is the perception of the connection between like and like, the Second Law is the application of judgment by means of definition or categorisation on the grounds of non-affinity, and the Third Law encapsulates a system of deduction based on perfect syllogistic language structures.

M. JOURDAIN: ...Perhaps we'll save logic for a rainy day. Have you got anything more straightforward?

PROFESSOR OF PHILOSOPHY:
Ethics?

M. JOURDAIN: Ethics?

PROFESSOR OF PHILOSOPHY:
Yes.

M. JOURDAIN: Ethics is what?

PROFESSOR OF PHILOSOPHY:
Ethics is the study of moral choice. It is

about being good. It teaches us to control
our baser passions.

M. JOURDAIN: No thanks. I am a hot-blooded chap, and
I fully intend to let my baser passions out
of the bag if I get the opportunity.

PROFESSOR OF PHILOSOPHY:
It could be the thing for you is physics.

M. JOURDAIN: Tell me about it.

PROFESSOR OF PHILOSOPHY:
We require physics to explain to us how
the world works. To define the properties
of matter and the principles of natural
phenomena. It covers all the elements:
metal, minerals, precious and semi-
precious stones, plants, and animals;
and it reveals to us the first causes of
meteors, rainbow, St. Elmo's fire, comets,
whirlwinds, thunder and lightning, rain,
snow, hail, storm and tempest.

M. JOURDAIN: No, life's too short.

PROFESSOR OF PHILOSOPHY:
What, then, may I teach you...?

M. JOURDAIN: Teach me to spell.

PROFESSOR OF PHILOSOPHY:
With the greatest pleasure. But we must
approach the subject philosophically.
Therefore, to start with let us consider,
what is the precise nature of the letters
of the alphabet? What are the differing
systems of pronunciation which we
may order from the mouth? To make
this clearer let me explain to you that
all letters are divided into vowels and
consonants. Vowels express the great

variety of sounds on offer and consonants come in between them. There are five vowels: A, E, I, O and U. *(Use French vowel sounds.)*

M. JOURDAIN: God, I never knew that.

PROFESSOR OF PHILOSOPHY:

You form the vowel A by opening the mouth wide, so: Ah. To make an E, bring the bottom jaw up towards the top one: Eh. For an I, narrow the gap between the jaws and direct the corners of the mouth in a straight line towards the centre of the ears: Eee. As if you were smiling. If you require an O you will find you have to open the mouth wide again and then bend in the lips at the corners: Oh. You will find it quite easy to memorise this one because it you are doing it correctly the mouth forms the same shape as the letter itself.

M. JOURDAIN: O. This is fascinating. O. Hooray for science.

PROFESSOR OF PHILOSOPHY:

The vowel U is pronounced by clenching the teeth – but not quite all the way – and then manipulating the lips forward in such a protuberant manner that it might be construed you meant to give someone a kiss. U.

M. JOURDAIN: U. Incredible! It works! Isn't life beautiful?

PROFESSOR OF PHILOSOPHY:

Tomorrow we shall advance to the consonants.

M. JOURDAIN: I hope they're as intriguing as these little beggars. O, O, O, U, U, U . . .

PROFESSOR OF PHILOSOPHY:
I will explain to you the secrets of language in all of its wealth and complexity.

M. JOURDAIN: Great. Now I'll let you into a secret of my own. I am in love with a lady – a noble lady – and I would like you to help me write a little note which I can drop at her dainty feet.

PROFESSOR OF PHILOSOPHY:
By all means.

M. JOURDAIN: That would be a pretty chic thing to do, wouldn't it?

PROFESSOR OF PHILOSOPHY:
Undoubtedly. Presumably you want it written in verse?

M. JOURDAIN: Verse? No. Can't stand verse.

PROFESSOR OF PHILOSOPHY:
In prose, then.

M. JOURDAIN: What do you think I am? Prose? Not bloody likely.

PROFESSOR OF PHILOSOPHY:
Well, I'm sorry, but it has to be one of the other. You can only express yourself in prose or verse.

M. JOURDAIN: What, piss-all else? Just prose or verse?

PROFESSOR OF PHILOSOPHY:
Yes.

M. JOURDAIN: That's a bit of a let-down. Call yourself a philosopher?

PROFESSOR OF PHILOSOPHY:

Whatever is not prose, is verse; and whatever is not verse, is prose.

M. JOURDAIN:

What about when I talk like I'm doing right at this moment, what's that then?

PROFESSOR OF PHILOSOPHY:

That, Monsieur, is prose.

M. JOURDAIN:

Are you telling me that when I say, "Nicole, fetch my slippers!" – that is prose?

PROFESSOR OF PHILOSOPHY:

I guarantee you it is.

M. JOURDAIN:

Stone me! You learn something new every day. You mean I've been talking in prose for forty bloody years and never known it? I am very, very grateful to you for bringing this matter to my attention. Now, I would like to say this in my letter: "Gorgeous Countess, your beautiful eyes make me die of love." But I want to put it more stylish than that.

PROFESSOR OF PHILOSOPHY:

Then say that the bonfire in her eyes has burnt you ardent heart to cinders, and that night after night you are tossing and –

M. JOURDAIN:

No, no, no, none of that flowery shit, thank you very much. I want exactly what I said: "Gorgeous Countess, your beautiful eyes make me die of love." But elegant.

PROFESSOR OF PHILOSOPHY:

I may need to extend the metaphor a touch.

M. JOURDAIN: You don't extend nothing. If anyone's doing any extending, it's me. Use just the words I have given you, but arrange them according to the fashion. Got it?

PROFESSOR OF PHILOSOPHY:
Then there are several options.
You may put it exactly as you did:
"Gorgeous Countess, your beautiful eyes make me die of love." Or you might try:
"Die of love, gorgeous Countess,
your beautiful eyes make me." Or:
"Your beautiful eyes, of love, gorgeous Countess, make me die." Or: "Eyes make me die, your beautiful gorgeous Countess, of love." Or: "Countess, love, die, make me, of your beautiful eyes!"

M. JOURDAIN: Which is best?

PROFESSOR OF PHILOSOPHY:
The original: "Gorgeous Countess, your beautiful eyes make me die of love."

M. JOURDAIN: Incredible. Though I've never studied linguistics, I still get it right first time. Many, many thanks, and please come again tomorrow. *(Exit the PROFESSOR OF PHILOSOPHY.)* Has my bastard suit arrived yet?

VALET: No, sir.

M. JOURDAIN: That bastard tailor wants his arse kicked. Keeping me waiting on such an important day! If the slimy old reptile was here now, I'd stitch up the crack in his – *(Enter the TAILOR, with his APPRENTICES bearing M. Jourdain's suit.)* Oh, there you are, at last. How nice to see you. I was just starting to get the tiniest impatient.

TAILOR:	I have had twenty apprentices at work all night on your suit. That accounts for the delay.
M. JOURDAIN:	These silk stockings you sent me are so tight I thought I would cut off the blood to my legs. And as for the shoes . . . ! They pinch!
TAILOR:	No they don't.
M. JOURDAIN:	They pinch! They hurt my feet!
TAILOR:	No, it's impossible.
M. JOURDAIN:	But I can feel pain now as I speak!
TAILOR:	I suppose you're going to tell me you've been walking in them.
M. JOURDAIN:	Well of course I've been walking in them!
TAILOR:	Well if you've been walking in them, what do you expect? This suit I have for you is a masterpiece. A formal garment, but in several contrapuntal colours. An innovation! Everybody at court will covet it.
M. JOURDAIN:	But look at this. You've got my fleurs-de-lys the wrong way up.
TAILOR:	No I haven't.
M. JOURDAIN:	Yes you have!
TAILOR:	You never said you wanted them the other way round.
M. JOURDAIN:	Is one meant to specify?
TAILOR:	Oh yes. But I'll have the whole lot altered for you. It'll only take another day and a night. Naturally you are aware that all the

	gentlemen at court are wearing them that way up this year.
M. JOURDAIN:	Are they?
TAILOR:	Certainly! – Don't you keep abreast of the collections?
M. JOURDAIN:	In that case leave it as it is.
TAILOR:	It's no trouble. Monsieur is always right.
M. JOURDAIN:	No! Just – leave it. Is this suit really me, do you think?
TAILOR:	It is more you than you are yourself.
M. JOURDAIN:	Are the wig and feathers still in fashion?
TAILOR:	A wig like that never goes out of fashion.
M. JOURDAIN:	*(Peering at the Tailor's suit.)* That fabric looks precisely the same as the last suit you made up for me.
TAILOR:	It looked so splendid on you, Monsieur, I could not resist.
M. JOURDAIN:	From my material? Are you looking for a kick in the nuts?
TAILOR:	Why don't you try on your handsome new suit?
M. JOURDAIN:	Righto, hand it over.
TAILOR:	No no no! A procedure exists, therefore it must be followed. My staff will dress you with appropriate ceremony. – Come forward! Attire Monsieur Jourdain in this creation exactly as you would clothe the greatest aristocrat in all France! *(Music. THE TAILOR'S APPRENTICES dance and dress M. JOURDAIN in his new clothes. He parades up and down.)*

APPRENTICE: Spare something for the lads to have a drink, Your Worship?

M. JOURDAIN: What did you call me?

APPRENTICE: I called you Your Worship, Your Worship.

M. JOURDAIN: Your Worship! That what you get for dressing like a class person, a person of rank. Walk round town dressed like a bourgeois and see how much respect you command. Here, that's for your Your Worship.

APPRENTICE: Thanks a lot, My Lord.

M. JOURDAIN: My Lord! That's quite a thing to be called. My Lord! That's worth a little bit extra. My Lord gives you this for your courtesy.

APPRENTICE: My Lord, with this we shall toast Your Grace's health.

M. JOURDAIN: Your Grace! Aah! Aah! Your Grace! I can't stand it! Don't go away. *(Aside.)* If he goes up to Your Majesty he'll get the whole purse. – Take this from Your Grace.

APPRENTICE: You're very generous, Monsieur. *(Exit the TAILOR and his APPRENTICES.)*

M. JOURDAIN: – Well that's a relief. Cheeky bugger nearly got the lot. *(To his VALETS.)* I intend to let the town get a good close look at my suit. Stay right behind me so that everyone sees you are mine.

VALETS: Yes, sir.

M. JOURDAIN: But first, where's Nicole? I ought to give her her instructions for the day. Nicole!

(NICOLE enters and immediately bursts out laughing at the sight of M. JOURDAIN.) Hush and listen. . . I want the whole place to be – Listen to me!. . . What's so bloody funny, Nicole?. . . What's got into the stupid girl? *(NICOLE simply cannot stop laughing.)*

NICOLE: It's – oh no it's too much – it's that outfit! Ha ha ha!

M. JOURDAIN: What about it?

NICOLE: Oh Jesus I can't stop meself . . .

M. JOURDAIN: Are you laughing at me, you fat tart?

NICOLE: Oh no sir. I wouldn't dare. Ha ha ha!

M. JOURDAIN: I should hope not, because if I discover that you are I shall slap your backside for you.

NICOLE: I'm sorry, I just can't help it, you do look so darn funny!

M. JOURDAIN: Oh I do, do I? Well I'm telling you now, Nicole, if you don't stop this ridiculous giggling I'm going to give you the thrashing of your life!

NICOLE: Good, good, that's cured it. I shan't be laughing no more now, sir.

M. JOURDAIN: At last. Will you please make sure that the salon is correctly –

NICOLE: *(Bursts out laughing again.)* Jesus Mary and Joseph the man's cracked! Ha ha ha!

M. JOURDAIN: I want everything cleaned and the silver polished for the –

NICOLE: Oh God I think I'll bust a gut! Ha ha ha!

M. JOURDAIN: Listen to my orders!

NICOLE: Sir, you'd better just hit me and get it over with, for I can't stop laughing, and it's doing me a power of good. Hit me now so I can laugh some more.

M. JOURDAIN: Insolence! Sauce and insolence!

NICOLE: Oh, please, let me laugh or I'll die!

M. JOURDAIN: I'm very nearly totally flaming furious, Nicole!

NICOLE: Ha ha ha! What job are you wanting me to start?

M. JOURDAIN: Well what do you think, you great slack slut? Put my house in good order for the polite company who will shortly be arriving.

NICOLE: Ah, shite. I can't laugh no more. The very words 'polite company' have me down in the dumps. Nobody makes more of a mess of a well-kept house than 'polite company'.

M. JOURDAIN: What am I supposed to do, slam the door in their faces?

NICOLE: There are certain faces would be improved by having the door slammed in them. *(Enter MME. JOURDAIN.)*

MME. JOURDAIN: I see we have begun a new chapter in the history of folly. What do you call that paraphernalia, husband? Do you want the entire world to laugh at you?

M. JOURDAIN: None but fools will laugh at me.

MME. JOURDAIN:	Then the entire world is composed of fools, for it's been laughing at you for a very long time.
M. JOURDAIN:	Please inform me, dearest wife, of whom these people are?
MME. JOURDAIN:	Anyone with a sound head on their shoulders, basically. Unlike you. The way you are living at present is a disgrace. What's got into you? I hardly know my own house. Every day is like a carnival. This morning there were enough dancers, singers and buskers in the courtyard to wake up the rest of the street.
NICOLE:	Madame is telling God's truth. How can I keep the household straight with that pack of rich layabouts you do forever invite in? Their shoes seem to search out the filthiest shite from the worst parts of town, and bring it back here and deposit it.
M. JOURDAIN:	Nicole, you are a peasant, shut up.
MME. JOURDAIN:	Nicole's quite right, and she thinks a lot clearer than you. Which is hardly difficult. Please enlighten me as to exactly what you want with a dancing master, at your age?
NICOLE:	Yes, and with that great boob of a fencing instructor who comes rattling through the house. The tiles on the walls shake loose when he goes by!
M. JOURDAIN:	Wife, shut up. Maid, shut up.
MME. JOURDAIN:	You'll have finally learnt to dance about the time your legs give out, won't you.

NICOLE: And would you skewer some poor soul with your rapier before you pass away?

M. JOURDAIN: Yes, you, if you don't belt up. Ignorant females. The advantages of my new social skills are clearly quite beyond you. And acquiring them takes some bloody effort!

MME. JOURDAIN: Your daughter is of an age when she ought to be provided with a husband. Why don't you put some effort into that?

M. JOURDAIN: When an acceptable match appears on the horizon, I'll marry her off. Meanwhile I am devoting myself to a life of scholarly pursuits.

NICOLE: 'Tis said, Madame, another clown signed up for the circus today: a Professor of Philosophy.

M. JOURDAIN: I want to improve my mind. I want to feel at ease in civilised company.

MME. JOURDAIN: You should go back to school. You'd get whipped.

M. JOURDAIN: By God, if I could learn what they teach in school, I'd take the whipping here and now. There's so much I don't know. What are you talking right this second for example?

MME. JOURDAIN: I'm talking sense. What are you talking? Claptrap.

M. JOURDAIN: I'm not talking about that kind of talking. I'm talking about talking in the sense of talking philosophically. Philosophically speaking, what sort of speech do you think you are saying?

MME. JOURDAIN:	I'm saying you should come back to the bosom of your family and live a decent life. Is that a suitable speech for the occasion?
M. JOURDAIN:	I don't mean that! That's ethics! I mean the words! These words I deftly formulate in my mouth – what are they composed of?
MME. JOURDAIN:	Wind.
M. JOURDAIN:	Try to be serious for thirty seconds. The language we are using at this moment in time. What is it?
MME. JOURDAIN:	You tell me.
M. JOURDAIN:	Very well, thickhead, I will. It's prose.
MME. JOURDAIN:	Prose?
M. JOURDAIN:	Prose. Anything that's prose cannot be verse and anything that's verse cannot be prose so there you are. Already I have immersed myself in the mainstream of current academic thought, and see how the windows have opened. Hey, Nicole, what do you do to say a U?
NICOLE:	What?
M. JOURDAIN:	What do you do to say a U?
NICOLE:	Sure the man's daft.
M. JOURDAIN:	Say U.
NICOLE:	No trouble: U.
M. JOURDAIN:	There! You did it!
NICOLE:	What? All I said was U.
M. JOURDAIN:	Exactly! And how did you do the sound?

NICOLE:	I did do exactly as you did bid me do.
M. JOURDAIN:	. . . It's like trying to bring intellectual light and purity to a flock of flaming sheep. – You clenched your teeth, Nicole, you clenched your teeth, but not fully, and then you manipulated your fat lips forward just as if you were going to give me a huge wet kiss, and then you said a U. See, I go to kiss, and: U.
NICOLE:	Kiss, and: U.
MME. JOURDAIN:	Extraordinary.
M. JOURDAIN:	Wait till you get your mouth round an O. And those cunning little consonants! You'll never believe it.
MME. JOURDAIN:	What is all this pigswill?
NICOLE:	Is there anything in it for plain simple folks?
M. JOURDAIN:	Imbecilic women! You drive me round the bend!
MME. JOURDAIN:	Get rid of these crackpot friends of yours, immediately!
NICOLE:	Specially that filthy, beastly, dirty swordsman.
M. JOURDAIN:	He really gets up your nose, doesn't he? Allow me to teach you some respect for his glorious trade. Bring the foils! *(The foils are brought and he gives one to NICOLE.)* Got a hold of it? Right. Reductive logic. Once you have lined yourself up straight it's simple. Lunge in quart, one, two, and in tierce, one, two, and repose. A subtle flick of the wrist will ensure you can never be killed. Which I must say

I find reassuring. Now, Nicole, take
a poke at me and I'll give a practical
demonstration. Go on, girl. En garde!
(NICOLE lunges and hits him several times.)

NICOLE: Like that?

M. JOURDAIN: Hey, no, hang on, stop! Oh blast the
bitch.

NICOLE: Just following orders.

M. JOURDAIN: Yes, all right, but you led in tierce before
you led in quart and confused me on
which one to parry.

MME. JOURDAIN: Husband, you have completely lost your
head. You are living in a fantasy world.
This comes from hob-nobbing with the
nobility, doesn't it?

M. JOURDAIN: Yes, darling one, thus revealing my
judgment of character to be infinitely
superior to those who only hob-nob with
the bourgeoisie.

MME. JOURDAIN: I hope you're not referring to your
judgment of the character of the sponging
Count you're in so thick with.

M. JOURDAIN: Christ, you are so tight-arsed! Count
Dorante holds a very high position at
court. You don't realise what a favourite
he is. He speaks to the King with as much
familiarity as I'm speaking to you now,
you silly cow! To Louis Quatorze! And
then he comes to my house and speaks to
me. Calls me his dearest friend. In front
of anyone who'll listen. He treats me as
an equal. His kindness knows no bounds.

MME. JOURDAIN: Nor his capacity for borrowing money.

M. JOURDAIN: It is an honour and a privilege to lend money to a gentleman of quality. Jesus, it's only money.

MME. JOURDAIN: And what do you get in return?

M. JOURDAIN: If you only knew.

MME. JOURDAIN: Pardon?

M. JOURDAIN: A business matter. Too complicated to explain. Besides, he has given me his word that he will pay me back.

MME. JOURDAIN: And you fell for it?

M. JOURDAIN: His word as a gentleman.!

MME. JOURDAIN: Pure rot.

NICOLE: He's coming in the door!

MME. JOURDAIN: On the scrounge again, no doubt. I'm sick to death of the man. *(Enter DORANTE.)*

DORANTE: Monsieur Jourdain, my friend. How are you?

M. JOURDAIN: I am very well, sir, thank you, and at your service.

DORANTE: And Madame Jourdain is also, I trust, very well?

M. JOURDAIN: She doesn't complain.

DORANTE: Why, Monsieur, we are making a serious sartorial statement today, are we not?

M. JOURDAIN: Oh, just flung on the first thing that came to hand, you know . . .

43

DORANTE: But it's stunning. None of the young gallants at court dresses as arrestingly as you.

M. JOURDAIN: Really?

MME. JOURDAIN: *(To NICOLE.)* Straight to his weak spot.

DORANTE: Do a little twirl for me. Oh, my. Altogether captivating.

MME. JOURDAIN: *(To NICOLE.)* Looks as soppy behind as in front.

DORANTE: My God, Jourdain, it does me good to see you. You're the one man in the world that I genuinely treasure, and I was saying something to that effect in the Royal Bedchamber this morning.

M. JOURDAIN: You do me a great honour, sir. *(To MME. JOURDAIN.)* The Royal Bedchamber!

DORANTE: Now please, replace your hat. We need not be too formal, you and I.

M. JOURDAIN: But Monsieur, I know I should show my respect.

DORANTE: To hell with etiquette. We're friends. Put on your hat.

M. JOURDAIN: I remain your servant, sir.

DORANTE: Look, I can't put on my hat until you put on yours, can I? Balance the damned thing upon your head.

M. JOURDAIN: *(Puts on his hat.)* It's very bad manners.

DORANTE: Monsieur, I am in debt to you. This I think you know.

MME. JOURDAIN: Yes, we know, we know.

DORANTE: On a number of occasions you have lent me money. And with the best grace in the world, I might add. But I know how to square my accounts, and I always return a favour done by a friend.

M. JOURDAIN: Naturally. Any gentleman does.

DORANTE: Therefore I have come to settle up with you.

M. JOURDAIN: Sorry?

DORANTE: I wish to pay you back.

M. JOURDAIN: *(To MME. JOURDAIN.)* Hear that? After all your stupid squawking?

DORANTE: I am the kind of person who believes in redeeming a loan at the earliest opportunity.

M. JOURDAIN: *(To MME. JOURDAIN.)* What did I tell you?

DORANTE: So – shall we take a peep at the running total?

M. JOURDAIN: *(To MME. JOURDAIN.)* Suspicious old witch.

DORANTE: Presumably you can recall the amounts you have lent me?

M. JOURDAIN: Yes I think so. I've kept a rough tally. Here it is. On the first occasion it was two hundred louis.

DORANTE: That's correct.

M. JOURDAIN: Next time, a hundred and twenty.

DORANTE: A hundred and twenty, yes.

M. JOURDAIN: Another time, a hundred and forty.

DORANTE: Correct.

M. JOURDAIN: Totalling four hundred and sixty louis,
that is, five thousand and sixty francs.

DORANTE: Your arithmetic's very good. Five
thousand and sixty francs. Fine.

M. JOURDAIN: Then one thousand eight hundred and
thirty-two francs to your plume-designer.

DORANTE: Agreed.

M. JOURDAIN: Two thousand seven hundred and eighty
to your tailor.

DORANTE: Him, yes.

M. JOURDAIN: Four thousand three hundred and
seventy-nine francs, twelve sous and eight
deniers to your caterers.

DORANTE: Twelve sous and eight deniers, remember
them well.

M. JOURDAIN: And one thousand seven hundred and
forty-eight francs, seven sous and four
deniers to your saddler.

DORANTE: So tell me the worst.

M. JOURDAIN: Grand total: fifteen thousand eight
hundred francs.

DORANTE: That's damned efficient book-keeping, sir.
Fifteen thousand eight hundred francs,
and if you just add on the two hundred
louis you're letting me have today, that'll
bring it up to a nice round eighteen
thousand, which I shall repay in full at
the first opportunity.

MME. JOURDAIN: Ha! Exactly as I suspected.

M. JOURDAIN: Hush!

DORANTE: That won't inconvenience you, will it?

M. JOURDAIN: Good lord, no.

MME. JOURDAIN: He milks you like a cow.

DORANTE: Any problem, I can always go elsewhere.

M. JOURDAIN: I won't hear of it, Monsieur.

MME. JOURDAIN: He'll not be content till he's bled you dry.

M. JOURDAIN: I've told you –

MME. JOURDAIN: He's a leech.

M. JOURDAIN: Shut your face.

MME. JOURDAIN: He'll suck out your very last sou.

M. JOURDAIN: Shut up! Please shut up!

DORANTE: I know stacks of people who could stump up a small sum like that. But since you are my best friend in the whole world, I thought you'd probably be rather miffed if I asked anyone else.

M. JOURDAIN: Quite right. What are friends for? I'll go straight out to the strongbox for you now.

MME. JOURDAIN: You fool. You're not actually giving him more, are you?

M. JOURDAIN: How can I refuse a gentleman who so cordially mentions my name in the King's bedroom? *(Exit M. JOURDAIN.)*

DORANTE: You do seem awfully gloomy today, Madame Jourdain. The world's not such a frightful place, is it?

MME. JOURDAIN: No?

DORANTE: But then your charming daughter is nowhere to be seen. Why's that, pray?

MME. JOURDAIN:	Because she's a lot better off somewhere else.
DORANTE:	How is she getting along these days?
MME. JOURDAIN:	On her legs.
DORANTE:	Perhaps you and she would care to accompany me to see the theatre and the ballet when next they play in the royal presence?
MME. JOURDAIN:	Oh yes please. We haven't had a laugh for a very long time. A very long time indeed.
DORANTE:	I would lay money on your having had more than your fair share of admirers, Madame Jourdain, in your youth, when you must have been terrifically beautiful and good-natured . . . ?
MME. JOURDAIN:	I'm a decrepit old harridan, now, is that what you're saying?
DORANTE:	Damnation! I do beg your pardon. Had I looked more closely, I should have seen of course that Madame's in the peak of condition even after all this time. What an impertinent dog I am! *(Enter M. JOURDAIN.)*
M. JOURDAIN:	I have here precisely two hundred louis.
DORANTE:	Jourdain, I am your servant for life. Let me know if there's any little favour I can do for you at court, won't you?
M. JOURDAIN:	That's very decent of you.
DORANTE:	If your dear wife would care to watch one of the royal *divertissements*, I can guarantee her the best seats in the house.

MME. JOURDAIN: His dear wife has an extremely hectic social calendar already. Tomorrow I bake. Next day: laundry. Day after that – *(DORANTE takes M. JOURDAIN aside.)*

DORANTE: As my note I trust made clear, the delicious countess will be arriving later to dine with us and watch your ballet. And I finally persuaded her to accept that diamond. Hell of a job getting her to take it. Jolly scrupulous lady. Only relented this very morning, as a matter of fact.

M. JOURDAIN: What did she make of it?

DORANTE: She adored it. Adored it. It's such a fabulous stone, I daresay it will vastly improve your standing in her sight.

M. JOURDAIN: God I hope so!

MME. JOURDAIN: *(To NICOLE.)* Once those two get yakking, you simply can't prise them apart.

DORANTE: I made sure that she's fully aware of the value of your gift – and, Monsieur, of the heat of your passion.

M. JOURDAIN: I can't comprehend why such a distinguished gentleman as yourself would want to descend to my piddling level and help out with my affairs.

DORANTE: You'd do the same for me, I know. Why should we allow any boring social barriers to stand between us? We are friends.

MME. JOURDAIN: *(To NICOLE.)* He makes me spew.

DORANTE: When a friend comes to one as you did and bares his soul, confesses his ardour for a strikingly beautiful person

whom one happens to know socially,
one has little choice but to intervene
and strive to bring the affair to a happy
consummation.

MME. JOURDAIN: *(To NICOLE.)* How long do I have to put
up with this?

NICOLE: They're practically down each others'
trousers.

DORANTE: Now, you've made a good start. The road
to her heart is wide open, because all
women love to be spoiled. The serenades
sung outside her window, the bouquets
of roses, the stunning fireworks display
on the ornamental lake, the gigantic
diamond, and today's I hope lavish and
spectacular entertainment will all speak
love to her so much better than words
ever could. Yours, anyway.

M. JOURDAIN: Nothing arouses me more than a lady of
genuine breeding. I want her and I don't
care what it costs.

MME. JOURDAIN: *(To NICOLE.)* What are they cooking up
together? Creep over and see if you can
find out.

DORANTE: Soon you will have the opportunity of
undressing her with your eyes . . .

M. JOURDAIN: To get a clear run at it, I'm packing my
wife off to her sister's for the rest of the
day.

DORANTE: How shrewd. Your wife is a woman who
has never quite grasped the concept
of pleasure. *(M. JOURDAIN sees NICOLE
eavesdropping, and hits her.)*

M. JOURDAIN: Piss off! Cheeky bint! – Let us take a breath of air, Monsieur. *(Exit M. JOURDAIN and DORANTE.)*

NICOLE: He's a devil! That's all you get for your curiosity: bruises. I fancy they're up to some naughty business, Madame, and they want you got out of the way.

MME. JOURDAIN: It's not the first time my husband has excited my suspicions. I think he's having an affair. Well, we'll see about *that*. But I want a word with you now on the matter of my daughter. You know Cléonte's in love with her. He's a good boy, he's clean in himself, he's got interests, and if I can I'd like to get him Lucile's hand in marriage.

NICOLE: God protect you, Madame, you couldn't have said a better thing than at all. 'Cause if you're pleased with the master, well, I'm a bit stuck on his man. Wouldn't it be wonderful if we could be wed stood right in the shadow of them! Like a fairytale, it'd be!

MME. JOURDAIN: Go and inform Cléonte of my intentions, then bring him back here and we'll tackle my husband together.

NICOLE: I never had a nicer job in my life! *(Exit MME. JOURDAIN. Enter CLÉONTE and COVIELLE.)* Oh, there you are, thanks be to God. I've terrific news for you, and I –

CLÉONTE: Get out of here, you dirty cheat. We don't want to hear any more of your hypocrisy.

NICOLE: What kind of welcome's that?

CLÉONTE: Get away, I said, and tell your rotten
            deceitful mistress that she'll never again
            make a fool of Cléonte, who trusted her
            far, far too much.

NICOLE: What has upset him so? Sweet Covielle,
            tell me what it's all about.

COVIELLE: Sweet Covielle nothing. Go away and
            never darken my eyesight again. Slag. Or
            speak to me or nothing.

NICOLE: *(Aside.)* Him as well? So what's put the
            wind up the boyos, I wonder? I had
            better run and tell the mademoiselle.
            (Exit NICOLE.)

CLÉONTE: What a way to treat the most passionate,
            faithful lover that ever walked the earth.

COVIELLE: Yes. Me too.

CLÉONTE: After I've shown the woman all the
            tenderness and devotion you could
            possibly imagine.

COVIELLE: Me too.

CLÉONTE: I don't talk to anyone else, I don't think
            about anyone else, she inhabits my most
            secret soul. She is my desire and my joy,
            the beat of my heart. And how does she
            repay me for this absolute commitment?
            Two days pass – or two millennia, I no
            longer know the difference – and we
            meet by chance. My heart goes beserk
            when I see her, utter rapture is written
            on my face, I stagger romantically in her
            direction, and the faithless witch walks
            past like I just don't exist.

COVIELLE: Me too.

CLÉONTE:	Did you ever see a cow like Lucile, Covielle?
COVIELLE:	Did you ever see a slag like Nicole, sir?
CLÉONTE:	After all my sacrifices, my sighs, my vows …!
COVIELLE:	After all the mucky jobs I've done in her kitchen.
CLÉONTE:	All the tears I've cried in her lap.
COVIELLE:	All the buckets I've drawn from her well.
CLÉONTE:	The fire in my bosom!
COVIELLE:	The heat of her oven!
CLÉONTE:	Now she treats me with contempt. She deserves to be roundly chastised for her perfidious treason.
COVIELLE:	My one's looking for a thrashing, too.
CLÉONTE:	Never speak to me of Lucile again, Covielle.
COVIELLE:	Wouldn't dream of it.
CLÉONTE:	Don't try and excuse her behaviour.
COVIELLE:	Don't worry.
CLÉONTE:	I shall lick my wounds in silence, and never, ever acknowledge the existence of the creature again.
COVIELLE:	Sound idea.
CLÉONTE:	Perhaps it's that raffish Count who's always loitering round here? Perhaps he's caught her eye? Such a capricious girl would obviously be swept straight off her feet by the promise of wealth and high

status. If so, honour requires that I move first, and ditch her before she ditches me.

COVIELLE: Hold tight to your self-respect, sir, that's what I'm doing.

CLÉONTE: I must root out every last lingering vestige of love for the vixen. You can help me by telling me all the rotten, horrid things you can recall about her. Catalogue her disgusting habits. Paint me a picture of her hideousness. I've got to make myself hate her.

COVIELLE: Shouldn't be too difficult. I don't know why you fell for Lucile in the first place. She's so pretentious! She's got cotton wool for brains. And her eyes are like two piss-holes in the snow.

CLÉONTE: Yes, she has dark little eyes. But how they glitter, how they sparkle, how they burn with true love's fire . . . !

COVIELLE: She's got a huge great mouth, though.

CLÉONTE: That's true. But then again you've never kissed it. Heaven.

COVIELLE: She's not very tall.

CLÉONTE: No, but her deportment is excellent.

COVIELLE: What about her silly, girly wit?

CLÉONTE: Oh, it's divine! So subtle and quick.

COVIELLE: Conversation?

CLÉONTE: Utterly charming.

COVIELLE: Though she's always so serious.

CLÉONTE: Oh, you like them flippant? I don't.

COVIELLE:	But this one changes her excuse for a mind more than any tart since time began!
CLÉONTE:	Yes, she does. Beautiful women are entitled to. A man just has to learn to live with it.
COVIELLE:	Sir. . . I don't quite know how to put this, but. . .you're hopelessly in love.
CLÉONTE:	Hell, am I? No, it's impossible. All that was love is turned to hate. I hate her. Hate.
COVIELLE:	I don't see how you can do so. You think she's perfect.
CLÉONTE:	Then let that be my most brilliant revenge; through sheer force of will I shall hate her, despise her, and leave her, even though I know she's the most magnificent woman I've ever met. *(Enter NICOLE and LUCILE.)*
NICOLE:	I was scandalised, honest and truly.
LUCILE:	It can only have been caused by you know what. Ah, here he is.
CLÉONTE:	I shan't speak to her at all.
COVIELLE:	Me neither.
LUCILE:	Whatever is the matter, Cléonte?
NICOLE:	And what's up with you, Covielle?
LUCILE:	What's made you angry?
NICOLE:	Why the black looks?
LUCILE:	Cat got your tongue, Cléonte?
CLÉONTE:	Jezebel!

LUCILE:	Yes dear, you're upset about earlier on, I know.
CLÉONTE:	Ah-hah! They are cognisant of their sin.
LUCILE:	This foul humour is all brought on by my demeanour when we passed in the park, isn't it?
CLÉONTE:	Yes, traitor, if I absolutely must speak to you, it is. And don't think for one single moment that I'm going to allow you the satisfaction of unceremoniously dumping me, because, Mademoiselle, I am unceremoniously dumping you first. It will take me a long time to get over you but the pain will be exquisite. And don't think I'll change my mind, either, because I would rip out my heart and devour it rather than be so wet as to crawl back to you.
COVIELLE:	Me too.
LUCILE:	This is a lot of fuss about nothing, Cléonte. May I please explain why I avoided your eyes this morning?
CLÉONTE:	No, I'm not listening.
NICOLE:	Covielle, there's a reason why we passed by so quick.
COVIELLE:	I'm not listening either.
LUCILE:	When we met –
CLÉONTE:	Said no, didn't I?
NICOLE:	'Twas like this –
COVIELLE:	I've gone deaf.
LUCILE:	Cléonte.

NICOLE: Covielle.

LUCILE: Just one word!

CLÉONTE: No!

NICOLE: Be reasonable!

COVIELLE: You're joking!

CLÉONTE: Leave us alone!

LUCILE: Fair enough then. If neither of you are
              prepared to listen to what we have to say,
              you can believe what you like, we can't
              be bothered.

NICOLE: In other words, stick it up your bum.

CLÉONTE: Wait. Tell us. Very briefly. Why did we
              get such a damn cool reception?

LUCILE: No, I no longer feel like it.

COVIELLE: Come on, tell us the story.

NICOLE: Nor do I feel like it, so there.

CLÉONTE: Please tell –

LUCILE: I'm sorry, I shan't.

COVIELLE: What about me?

NICOLE: You can go play with yourself.

CLÉONTE: Lucile.

COVIELLE: Nicole.

CLÉONTE: I beg you.

LUCILE: Hard luck.

COVIELLE: Give in.

NICOLE: Not a chance.

LUCILE:	Go away!
CLÉONTE:	Right, I shall! If this is the way I am treated! I shall go away and kill myself, and it will all be your fault, Lucile!
COVIELLE:	So will I.
LUCILE:	Don't be ridiculous, you couldn't kill yourself if you tried.
CLÉONTE:	Could.
LUCILE:	Couldn't.
CLÉONTE:	Could.
LUCILE:	Couldn't.
COVIELLE:	I could.
NICOLE:	Nobody's asking you.
LUCILE:	Had you the decency to listen to our explanation in the first place, the question would not have arisen! The problem this morning was caused by the presence of a crabby old aunt of mine, who believes that a girl is dishonoured if a man so much as smiles at her. She thinks all men are lechers, and should be avoided like the plague. She may be right. When out in her company I abide by her wishes.
NICOLE:	And so do I. There – you see?
CLÉONTE:	This isn't another elaborate tissue of deception, I sincerely hope, Lucile?
COVIELLE:	No little white lies, eh, Nicole?
LUCILE:	The truth. That's all.
NICOLE:	The truth.

COVIELLE: Shall we fall for it?

CLÉONTE: Oh, Lucile, my darling! One word from your inimitable mouth, and my broken heart is mended!

COVIELLE: All right, we'll fall for it. *(They embrace. Enter MME. JOURDAIN.)*

MME. JOURDAIN: I am very glad to see you, Cléonte. And this is first rate timing, because my husband's on his way. Seize the opportunity. Ask for Lucile's hand in marriage.

CLÉONTE: Madame, I have never entertained a more delightful suggestion. *(Enter M. JOURDAIN.)* Monsieur, I should like to come straight to the point and request of you something that I've been mulling over for some considerable time. I should like to ask you, and I have thought about this at great, almost indeterminate, length, whether you would do me the honour, and yourself the advantage, of accepting me, after all due and necessary processes, both ecclesiastical and civil, as your. . .son-in-law.

M. JOURDAIN: Before I give an answer to that, Monsieur, I should like to put something to you. Are you a gentleman by birth?

CLÉONTE: Monsieur, very few men would hesitate to answer that question in the affirmative. The title "gentleman" is worn carelessly these days, like an old felt hat in the rain. But I am more discriminating as to its usage. In my opinion it ill becomes an honest man to step out in the world under false pretences. It is undignified to disguise the circumstances of one's birth, and to pretend to something one is not. Therefore I must tell you that although I come from the most respectable stock, have served six years in the armed forces, and have at my disposal a perfectly decent yearly income, I will not assume a position to which I lack entitlement, and therefore, Monsieur, I must answer that no, I am not a gentleman by birth.

M. JOURDAIN: Then shake hands and be on your way, Monsieur. My daughter's not for you.

CLÉONTE: What?

M. JOURDAIN: You're not a gentleman; you don't get her.

MME. JOURDAIN: What do you know about gentlemen? You and me weren't exactly born with pure blue blood!

M. JOURDAIN: Hush, wife, I know the peculiar way your mind works.

MME. JOURDAIN: The pair of us come from the bourgeoisie. Shopkeeping stock!

M. JOURDAIN: Horse shit, you're talking horse shit as usual.

MME. JOURDAIN: Your father was a market trader, just like mine.

M. JOURDAIN: Sod the woman! Always the same silly tune. If your old man was a tradesman, that's your problem. But anyone who says the same about mine has been misinformed. I repeat for the last time: I intend to have a noble son-in-law.

MME. JOURDAIN: Our daughter ought to marry the man who's right for her, and far better for him to be an ordinary chap with money and reasonable looks, than some clapped-out specimen of the impoverished aristocracy!

NICOLE: And that's the truth. In my village the lord of the manor's son is the most revolting, useless cretin you ever laid eyes on.

M. JOURDAIN: Stop stirring it, yokel. My daughter is very well provided for; yet the one thing she lacks is a nice coat of arms. So, I intend to make her a marquise.

MME. JOURDAIN: A marquise!

M. JOURDAIN: Yes, a marquise!

MME. JOURDAIN: God forbid!

M. JOURDAIN: I am resolved for it.

MME. JOURDAIN: Well I am resolved against it. Marry above yourself and you get nothing but trouble, trouble and more trouble. I don't want to have a son-in-law who thinks his wife's parents are an embarrassment, nor do I want grandchildren who are ashamed to call me granny. I have this nightmare of my daughter coming to visit, as snooty as you like, and cold-shouldering the neighbours. Wouldn't their tongues start to wag! "Look at Jourdain's daughter," they'd snigger, "Madame la Marquise she is now, and isn't she full of herself? We were good enough for her when she was little, but now she's gone up in the world. Very high and mighty. Yet both her grandfathers sold cloth by St. Innocent's Gate, did you know that? Whether it was good, legitimate cloth, nobody could say- but whoever got rich by honest dealing?" I couldn't stand to have to listen to that gossip! I would like a man who was thankful to have got my dear daughter for his bride. Someone to who I could say, "Sit down there, son, and share our bite of dinner."

M. JOURDAIN: . . . If you want to stay in the gutter, stay in the gutter. I don't care if I have to take on the entire world, I will make my daughter a Marquise. And if I get any more lip, I'll make her an arseholing Duchess. *(Exit M. JOURDAIN.)*

MME. JOURDAIN: Have courage, Cléonte, there's still a chance. Lucile, come with me and we'll tell your father firmly that if you can't marry him, you won't marry anyone. You'll become a nun. *(Exit MME. JOURDAIN, LUCILE, and NICOLE.)*

COVIELLE: Well done. See where your high moral principles get you?

CLÉONTE: What else could I do? I am a man of honour.

COVIELLE: Yes, but he's not, is he? He's raving mad! You could have played along with this little charade.

CLÉONTE: I suppose so. But I never thought you'd need to show proofs of gentility to become the son-in-law of Monsieur Jourdain! *(COVIELLE starts to laugh.)* What's so damn funny about it?

COVIELLE: I've just had an idea.

CLÉONTE: For what?

COVIELLE: For getting you married to Miss Big-mouth. Oh, that's neat, that's really neat. And we'll take the piss out of Jourdain whilst we're at it. *(Laughing.)* I'm a genius! Come with me, sir, and I'll tell you what to do whilst I'm getting you ready.

CLÉONTE: This had better work, Covielle. *(Exit CLÉONTE and COVIELLE. Enter M. JOURDAIN, dressed to go hunting.)*

M. JOURDAIN: And what's wrong with getting a bit clubby with the upper class? All I am trying to do is acquire some social graces, and you don't acquire social graces from bloody plebs, do you? Wish I'd been born a Marquis. I'd give my entire fortune to've been born a sodding Marquis. *(Enter a VALET.)*

VALET: Sir, the Count is here, and a lady with him.

M. JOURDAIN: Christ! Already! I haven't finished yelling at my minions! Tell them I'll be right back. *(Exit M. JOURDAIN. Enter DORIMÈNE and DORANTE.)*

DORIMÈNE: I think this liaison is dangerous, Dorante. Letting you bring me to a house where I know not a soul. It is scarcely conventional behaviour.

DORANTE: Where then do you expect me to escort you, Madame, since you insist that neither your house nor my own is safe from scandal?

DORIMÈNE: Indeed – yet you fail to mention how I thus find myself drifting ever more steadily into the net of your desire. How I find myself accepting these extravagant presents as testimony of your love – I don't want them, palpably, but my resistance weakens in the face of your courtesy and charm. And how gradually I find myself succumbing to all your. . . . appetites. It began with the persistent visits to my salon. Next came the declarations of unyielding love, followed swiftly by the sumptuous gifts and entertainments, none of which interested me in the slightest as I made quite clear at the time, but all of which have contrived to enmesh me yet further in your grand design, your seductive intrigue, which I know must lead inexorably forward to the end I most resist: marriage.

DORANTE: Damn my eyes, you're as sharp as a blade. I will perforce be ruthlessly frank. You are a widow of independent means. I am my own man and I owe nothing to no-one and, most vital, I swear I love you more than the blood in my veins. It would make me monstrously happy if you would forget the disappointments of your last canter round the track and agree to wed me today.

DORIMÈNE: Two things unsettle me still, Dorante. One, that I am so caressed, so licked by the tongue of pleasure which your generosity extends that I am sucked in further than I might wish, and (b), that you can't afford it.

DORANTE: A detail. I never bother with –

DORIMÈNE: Well I do. I will not see you overspend on me. This diamond for instance must have cost a fortune.

DORANTE: Dorimène. . . No material value can be placed on my passion for you. And that bauble is unworthy of your beauty. I long to – but sadly here comes the master of the house. *(Enter M. JOURDAIN. He makes two spirited bows, and finds himself too close to DORIMÈNE.)*

M. JOURDAIN: Step backwards, would you, Madame?

DORIMÈNE: What on earth do you – ?

M. JOURDAIN: For the third bow. Just one pace astern – and, ah, nose –

DORIMÈNE: *(Moving.)* Really!

M. JOURDAIN: – level with knees – and voila!

DORANTE: Monsieur Jourdain is a stickler for etiquette, Madame.

M. JOURDAIN: Madame, I am greatly honoured to be fortunate enough to be so happy as to have the felicity of having you have the goodness of doing me the great honour of the favour of your presence in my house, and if I merit the merit of the merit of your . . . visit . . . then Heaven will . . . envying my good fortune . . . look down and . . . er, see . . . it.

DORANTE: Come, Monsieur, you will embarrass Madame. She knows you are a wit, a raconteur, a gallant; you need not labour the point. *(To DORIMÈNE.)* The simple bourgeois is sincere, but over-stretches himself, I think?

DORIMÈNE:	*(To DORANTE, with distaste.)* I think so too.
DORANTE:	Madame, Monsieur Jourdain is my dearest friend.
M. JOURDAIN:	The honour is more than I deserve.
DORANTE:	He is a gentleman of many parts.
DORIMÈNE:	Then I value his attributes highly.
M. JOURDAIN:	I've hardly started yet, Madame. You wait till I get going.
DORANTE:	*(To M. JOURDAIN.)* Don't make any reference to that jewel you gave her, will you?
M. JOURDAIN:	What? Can't I even ask her if she likes it?
DORANTE:	Absolutely not done. Not done at all. Considered rather vulgar as a matter of fact. The stylish thing would be to act as if you had no knowledge of it whatever. – Monsieur Jourdain, who is a trifle shy, was just saying, Madame, how delighted he is to see you grace his humble portals. *(To M. JOURDAIN.)* Devil of a job getting her to come, actually.
M. JOURDAIN:	Well thanks for all your trouble.
DORANTE:	He says, Madame, that he thinks you are the most beautiful woman he has ever seen.
DORIMÈNE:	He is extremely charming.
M. JOURDAIN:	No, no, it's you who is charming, Madame, and witty, and clever, and you smell very nice, and –
DORANTE:	I believe it is time for dinner.
VALET:	Everything's prepared, Monsieur.

DORANTE: Then let us be seated. And let's have some music! *(The COOKS bring in tables laden with food. As they serve, they sing and dance. DORIMÈNE, DORANTE and M. JOURDAIN sit down to eat.)*

COOKS' SONG

Refrain.

Hot from the kitchen,
Baked, sautéed or stewed;
Timeless, bewitching,
Ever renewed:
The splendour of food.

Solo.

The recipe for contentment's
Food and the prospect of love –
So dine today in perfect harmony.

Refrain.

Solo.

What better complements a wondrous dinner
Than brandy and wine and charming company?

Refrain.

END OF ACT ONE

ACT TWO

DORIMÈNE, DORANTE and M. JOURDAIN are still eating.

DORIMÈNE: This is a wonderful feast, Dorante!

M. JOURDAIN: Don't make fun of me, Madame. I only wish the cuisine was up to your usual standard.

DORANTE: Monsieur Jourdain is right for once. Although I am hugely obliged to him for his hospitality towards yourself, Madame, it cannot be denied that this meal is not worthy of you. It is I who am responsible for the preparation of the menu. But in the art of the table, I am somewhat unschooled. In consequence you may perchance detect a rather vile lack of sophistication in our gastronomy. If the great chef Damis were presiding over our refreshment today, everything would be presented according to the most precise culinary rituals. All would be elegance and formality – none of this mish-mash of colours and flavours. Damis would recite a verse over each dish as it was served, dazzling us with his skill in the science of good eating. He'd speak of the perfection of fresh-baked bread, its goodness locked in a golden crust, its crumbs going soft on the palate; of the body and bouquet of the wine, youthful and muscular but not too aggressive; of neck of lamb garnished with parsley; of a loin of Normandy veal, long and white, and sweet as almond paste; of spiced partridge; and finally of his famous crowning glory, a great plump turkey in a barley broth, adorned with onions, robed in chicory, and guarded by hand-killed pigeons. But I know nothing about cooking. So I can only agree with Jourdain, and wish he had treated you better.

DORIMÈNE: The only way I can satisfactorily reply to your compliments, Monsieur, is to eat just as much as I can.

M. JOURDAIN: Christ, you've got marvellous hands . . .

DORIMÈNE: Very ordinary hands, Jourdain, but if your eye has been caught by my diamond, why yes, it's a marvellous thing.

M. JOURDAIN: What is, Madame?

DORIMÈNE: My diamond.

M. JOURDAIN: Diamond? What diamond? – Oh, that. I hardly noticed it, but – do wear it if it gives you pleasure.

DORIMÈNE: You are very discriminating – not to say overparticular.

M. JOURDAIN: Thank you very much.

DORANTE: More wine for Monsieur Jourdain! Hurry up!

DORIMÈNE: And to season the food with dance and song, Dorante – so clever. So congenial. The entire meal has been quite lovely!

M. JOURDAIN: Not quite as lovely as you.

DORIMÈNE: Oh! Monsieur Jourdain is more lively that I expected!

DORANTE: Why, what did you expect from him?

M. JOURDAIN: I wish she'd expect me a bit later on.

DORIMÈNE: And again! Oh!

DORANTE: I'm afraid you don't know him properly, Madame.

M. JOURDAIN: She can explore the terrain any time she likes.

DORIMÈNE: I can't compete.

DORANTE: He has a smart answer to everything, hasn't he? Have you noticed how he eats the food you have spat out and left on your plate?

DORIMÈNE: Monsieur Jourdain tickles my fancy.

M. JOURDAIN: I'll tickle your fancy all right, and I'll tell you what with, too, if you'll – *(Enter MME. JOURDAIN.)*

MME. JOURDAIN: I see we have company. And someone neglected to send me an invitation. This is why I was dispatched to my sister's for lunch and a long siesta, was it, O matrimonial mistake? There's some sort of pantomime going on downstairs! And up here what do I find but a banquet fit for a society ball! What the dickens do you think you're playing at? Flirting with women whilst I'm up the road . . . ! How much did all this cost you?

DORANTE: Your husband has not spent his money. I have spent mine. My friend has generously lent me his house for the afternoon, that's all. Every once in a while I fear for your mental stability, Madame Jourdain. I think you may be suffering from the delusion that we all loathe the sight of your withered old husk.

M. JOURDAIN: That's right, you rude article! Count Dorante has simply done me the honour of inviting me to join him for dinner in the house he has borrowed from me, and to listen to my orchestra with him and his guest, who is a lady of high rank, and I'm not so unmannerly as to disoblige him.

MME. JOURDAIN: Pigswill. I've got eyes in my head.

DORANTE: Perhaps you need spectacles.

MME. JOURDAIN: I do not need ruddy spectacles! I see the situation with absolute clarity! I am not a beast of the yard, I have feelings! I would have thought it beneath a peer of the realm to be so wicked as to assist my clapped-out spouse with his bird-brained schemes. As for you, Madame, and your pedigree, was it never suggested to you back in the château that it might not be too polite to go round breaking up peoples' homes and letting peoples' half-baked husbands fall hopelessly in love with you?

DORIMÈNE: What? How bizarre. No doubt it is frightfully amusing, Dorante, to have me abused by this weird old eccentric, but I'm distressed that I don't get the joke. *(DORIMÈNE storms out.)*

DORANTE: Madame, wait! Where are you going?

M. JOURDAIN: Madame! My lord, please give her my apologies and try to bring her back! *(Exit DORANTE.)* Right, wife. Bilious, wizened wife. Do you see what you have done? These are proper people! And you have offended them and driven them out of my house.

MME. JOURDAIN: I don't give a toss. Proper people. Phaw!

M. JOURDAIN: Have you ever had a leg of pork wrapped round your ear? A parsnip up the snout? Because at this moment in time you are very, very close. You ruined this fabulous meal!

MME. JOURDAIN: I'd laugh if you weren't so pathetic. I have rights, you know. And every last woman will support me. *(Exit MME. JOURDAIN. The dinner table is removed.)*

M. JOURDAIN: Yes, go on, scuttle off out before I really get narked. – Well her bloody timing was perfect as usual. I was just warming up. I was about to ejaculate some terrific repartee. – Who the hell are you? *(Enter COVIELLE, disguised.)*

COVIELLE: I don't think you know me, Monsieur.

M. JOURDAIN: You're bloody right I don't.

COVIELLE: I knew you when you were no bigger than this.

M. JOURDAIN: Me?

COVIELLE: Yes, you. Oh, you were such a pretty baby. All the women used to pick you up and kiss you.

M. JOURDAIN: Kiss me? What, with their lips?

COVIELLE: Yes. I was actually very close to your most respected father whilst he was on the earth.

M. JOURDAIN: My most regretted father . . . ?

COVIELLE: Oh yes. A perfect gentleman, your father.

M. JOURDAIN: Pardon?

COVIELLE: I said he was a perfect gentleman. Your father.

M. JOURDAIN: My father?

COVIELLE: Your father.

M. JOURDAIN: Did you know him well?

COVIELLE: Very well indeed.

M. JOURDAIN: And you knew him to be a perfect . . . gentleman . . . of noble birth?

COVIELLE: No doubt about it.

M. JOURDAIN: People are bigots, aren't they? People are such bloody bigots.

COVIELLE: I'm not with you.

M. JOURDAIN: Well, there are some evil-minded bastards who have put it about that my dad was in trade.

COVIELLE: In trade! What a foul slander. Never in a million years. His greatest joy was to help folk out, not cheat them, good gracious no, and as he had the most encyclopaedic knowledge of ribbons and fabrics and stuff of that order, he would happily wander hither and thither across the town trying to find little strips for his collection, and if some friend or other happened to call at his house and see a length they really fancied, why, do you know, he'd let them have it for nothing. Just covered his out-of-pocket expenses.

M. JOURDAIN:	I am delighted to have made your acquaintance. Now I've a witness my dad was a toff. May I inquire, sir, what business brings you here?
COVIELLE:	Since the days when I was befriended by your late father – the nobleman – I have travelled to the end of the earth.
M. JOURDAIN:	To the end of the earth! Where's that?
COVIELLE:	It's a long way away.
M. JOURDAIN:	I bet it is. What's it like?
COVIELLE:	Very queer.
M. JOURDAIN:	Does it suddenly stop?
COVIELLE:	Didn't look. I returned four days ago, and I thought I better get along to you quick, for I've got some incredible news.
M. JOURDAIN:	Oh? What?
COVIELLE:	You know that the son of the Sultan of Turkey is here in town?
M. JOURDAIN:	No, I didn't know.
COVIELLE:	You didn't know? Where have you been hiding? He's got this fantastic entourage of servants and whatnot. Everybody's paid a courtesy call on him. He's been received in Paris as a personage of the very highest importance.
M. JOURDAIN:	Has he really? First I've heard of it.
COVIELLE:	Well, it's to your advantage, in fact, because he's fallen in love with your daughter.
M. JOURDAIN:	The son of the Sultan of Turkey?

COVIELLE: Yep, and he's hoping to become your son-in-law.

M. JOURDAIN: The son of the Sultan of Turkey is hoping to become my son-in-law?

COVIELLE: The son of the Sultan of Turkey is hoping to become your son-in-law. You catch on quick. Do you speak Turkish?

M. JOURDAIN: No!

COVIELLE: Well, luckily I do. I went to see him and we had a long chat and some of that coffee they drink. In the course of this conversation he said to me: "Acciam croc soler ouch moustaph gidelum amanahem varahini oussere carbulath." Which means: "Have you ever encountered the beautiful daughter of Monsieur Jourdain, a nobleman of Paris?"

M. JOURDAIN: The son of the Sultan of Turkey said that about me?

COVIELLE: In exactly those words. Of course I said I know you very well, and that I had been fortunate enough to catch a glimpse once of your daughter. Then he says: "Ah! Marababa sahem!" – meaning, "O I love her so."

M. JOURDAIN: "Marababa sahem!" means "O I love her so"?

COVIELLE: Yes.

M. JOURDAIN: Christ, I worship language! "Marababa sahem! Marababa sahem!" It's terrific.

COVIELLE: It's neat isn't it. What about this: "Cacaracamouchen." Guess what that means.

M. JOURDAIN: "Cacaracamouchen"? I can't.

COVIELLE: It means, "Dearest love."

M. JOURDAIN: "Cacaracamouchen" means "Dearest love"?

COVIELLE: Spot on.

M. JOURDAIN: Astonishing! Turkish will be very, very useful.

COVIELLE: I must conclude my role as ambassador. The Turk's coming here to ask for your daughter's hand in marriage. However, he wants to make sure that his father-in-law is of acceptable status before the off, so he intends to confer on you, sir, the title of "Mamamouchi", which is a great honour in his country.

M. JOURDAIN: "Mamamouchi"?

COVIELLE: "Mamamouchi". As we would say, a Paladin. You know what a Paladin is. It's one of the very ancient, mythical forms of . . . Paladin. There is not a rank more senior anywhere on the globe.

M. JOURDAIN: The son of the Sultan of Turkey is exceedingly gracious. If you would be so kind as to conduct me to his apartments, I will thank him personally.

COVIELLE: It is not necessary. I told you, he's coming here.

M. JOURDAIN: Here?

COVIELLE: Yes, and he's bringing all the accoutrements for the initiation ceremony.

M. JOURDAIN: Bit sudden, isn't it?

COVIELLE: *(Shrugs.)* He's in love.

M. JOURDAIN: There's only one thing that worries me. My daughter's as stubborn as a pig in shit. She's determined to marry some berk called Cléonte. She declares she will have no-one else.

COVIELLE: She'll change her mind when she sees the son of the Sultan of Turkey. By a remarkable coincidence, the son of the Sultan of Turkey bears a strong resemblance to this berk Cléonte.

M. JOURDAIN: How do you know Cléonte?

COVIELLE: I saw him weeping in the gutter by your gate as I come in. If she loves *him*, surely the power of her emotion for the son of the Sultan will be – hold up, here he is. *(Solemn music. Enter CLÉONTE in Turkish costume, with his ATTENDANTS, dressed up in ridiculous garb. No-one but M. JOURDAIN is fooled.)*

CLÉONTE: Ambousahim oqui boraf, Giourdina, salamelequi!

COVIELLE: He says, "Monsieur Jourdain, may your heart be like a blooming rose bush, all year round." This is a normal mode of address where he comes from.

M. JOURDAIN: I am the humble servant of His Imperial Turkish Majesty.

COVIELLE: Carigar camboto oustin moraf.

CLÉONTE: Oustin yoc catamelequi basum base alla moran.

COVIELLE: He says, "May heaven grant you the strength of the lion and the sagacity of the snake."

M. JOURDAIN: Please tell His Turkish Majesty that I wish him a lot of nice things.

COVIELLE: Ossa binamen sadoc bably oracaf ouram.

CLÉONTE: Bel men.

COVIELLE: He says would you please go with him straight away to prepare for the ceremony, in order that he may then be formally introduced to your daughter, and take her as his loving bride.

M. JOURDAIN: He said all that in two words?

COVIELLE: It's an extraordinary language. Two words, and the world is at your feet. Go along with him now.

M. JOURDAIN: Righto. *(Exit M. JOURDAIN and CLÉONTE.)*

COVIELLE: *(Laughs.)* What a wanker. *(Enter DORANTE.)* Monsieur, may I count on you to help me with my scheme?

DORANTE: Covielle? Is that you? What a damned outrageous costume!

COVIELLE: Bizarre, isn't it? It's part of a nifty device, what's meant to trick Monsieur Jourdain into marrying his girl to my master.

DORANTE: Well, you're two or three lengths ahead of me, Covielle. Devil of a task getting the old brain underway at this time of the afternoon, but do pray explain all the devious machinations of the plot.

COVIELLE:	It's a spectacle that'll appeal to you. Come over here and watch what happens. I'll fill you in on the background. *("The Turkish Ceremony," during which M. JOURDAIN is enobled. Music. Enter a number of dancing Turks and Dervishes. They are followed by the MUFTI. The MUFTI invokes Mahomet and the Turks make obeisance, chanting to Allah. The Dervishes lead in M. JOURDAIN, dressed in "Turkish" costume. The MUFTI chants in lingua franca.)*
MUFTI:	Mahametta, per Giourdina Mi pregar sera e mattina: Voler far un Paladina De Giourdina, de Giourdina. Dar turbanta, e dar scarcina, Con galera e brigantina, Per defender Palestina. Mahametta, per Giourdina Mi pregar sera e mattina. *(To the TURKS.)* E Giourdina con Mahametta?
TURKS:	Yes, by Allah! Yes he is!
MUFTI:	*(Dancing and chanting.)* Allah baba hou, Allah hou!
TURKS:	Allah baba hou, Allah hou! *(The DERVISHES place a copy of the Koran on M. JOURDAIN's back, and the MUFTI reads from it, in a mock ceremony.)*
MUFTI:	Ti non star furba?
TURKS:	No, no, no, Giourdina no heathen!
MUFTI:	Non star furfanta?

TURKS:	No, no, no, Giourdina no devil!
MUFTI:	Donar turbanta, donar turbanta! *(They place an enormous turban on M. JOURDAIN's head.)* Dara, dara, Bastonnara.
TURKS:	Bastonnara, bastonnara! *(They give M. JOURDAIN a ceremonial beating with this scimitars, and then raise him up. Now they dance for him – a wild, sensual dance. And the ceremony is concluded. The MUFTI bows to him.)*
MUFTI:	Giourdina. Mamamouchi. *(Exit the MUFTI and the TURKS. M. JOURDAIN is left dazed, bewildered and happy. Enter MME. JOURDAIN.)*
MME. JOURDAIN:	Oh, Lord! It's finally happened. His wits have deserted him. – Have you completely lost touch with reality, Jourdain? If not, why are you wearing half the contents of an Arabian laundry?
M. JOURDAIN:	Dozy bitch. How dare you speak like that to a Mamamouchi?
MME. JOURDAIN:	What are you raving about?
M. JOURDAIN:	You have to show me more respect now. I've been made a Mamamouchi.
MME. JOURDAIN:	What's Mamamouchi? A mushroom?
M. JOURDAIN:	No! A Mamamouchi is . . . it's like . . . well, I'm a Paladin in Turkey.
MME. JOURDAIN:	I know you're a turkey. You've always been a turkey. But what have you got on your head?

M. JOURDAIN:	The ignorance of the woman! This is a turban. I have just had the full ceremonial honours conferred on me.
MME. JOURDAIN:	What ceremonial honours?
M. JOURDAIN:	Mahametta per Giordina.
MME. JOURDAIN:	What's that mean?
M. JOURDAIN:	Mahametta, that's Mohamet – the god. Giourdina, that's Jourdain – me.
MME. JOURDAIN:	And what about Jourdain – you?
M. JOURDAIN:	Voler far un Paladina.
MME. JOURDAIN:	Why?
M. JOURDAIN:	Dar turbanta con galera.
MME. JOURDAIN:	You're not making a great deal of sense, dear.
M. JOURDAIN:	Per defender Palestina.
MME. JOURDAIN:	No, it's all complete rhubarb.
M. JOURDAIN:	Dara dara bastonnara! *(He begins to chant and dance.)*
MME. JOURDAIN:	Don't think that's going to make things any clearer.
M. JOURDAIN:	Allah baba hou, Allah hou!
MME. JOURDAIN:	Stop! You'll do yourself a mischief!
M. JOURDAIN:	Allah baba hou, Allah hou! *(He falls over.)*
MME. JOURDAIN:	What did I tell you? You're bonkers.
M. JOURDAIN:	Be silent! Show respect to a Mamamouchi! *(Exit M. JOURDAIN.)*
MME. JOURDAIN:	How did this happen? He's completely mad. I better keep him out of the sight

of the neighbours. – Oh, not those two troublemakers. It's chaos everywhere I look! *(Exit MME. JOURDAIN. Enter DORIMÈNE and DORANTE.)*

DORANTE: Madame, I wager it is quite the most amusing little pageant that you ever will have seen. The old boy looks such a fool! We must be careful not to give Cléonte away. He's a fine chap, deeply meritorious of our approbation and so forth.

DORIMÈNE: I have certainly found him so. He deserves good fortune.

DORANTE: Did you enjoy the entertainments, Dorimène?

DORIMÈNE: They were superb, Dorante. But I cannot put up with this state of affairs any longer. I must limit your prodigality or I fear you will be bankrupt in a month. I have decided that the only way to curtain such extravagance is to marry you immediately. That usually puts an end to it.

DORANTE: Oh! Madame . . . Have you really come to such a heavenly conclusion?

DORIMÈNE: Yes, but only to keep you from rack and ruin. If I don't move fast you won't have anything left, will you?

DORANTE: I thank you from the bottom of my soul for having such concern for my personal fortune. But I do assure you that there is absolutely nothing to worry about.

DORIMÈNE: Then I am content. Our host approaches. Doesn't he look splendid? *(Enter M. JOURDAIN.)*

DORANTE: Excellency, we have come to pay homage to your grand new station in life, and to rejoice with you in the forthcoming marriage of your daughter to the Son of the Sultan.

M. JOURDAIN: *(Bows in the Turkish manner.)* Monsieur, I wish you the strength of the snake and the intellect of the lion.

DORIMÈNE: May I be the first, your Excellency, to congratulate you on the glorious rank to which you have been so justly elevated?

M. JOURDAIN: Madame, I hope your rose-bud blossoms all year round. I am extremely gratified that you have returned to my palace, and I hope you will accept my humble apologies for the bloody disgraceful conduct of my repellent wife.

DORIMÈNE: I have already forgiven her her little outburst. It cannot be altogether easy, living in the shadow of a man of such prodigious qualities as yourself; and clearly your heart is most precious to her.

M. JOURDAIN: But my heart belongs to you.

DORANTE: You will apprehend, I hope, Madame, that Monsieur Jourdain is not one of those types who forget their good manners when they start going up in the world. Even from the loftiness of his exalted position, he remembers his love for his friends.

DORIMÈNE: It shows a true generosity of spirit.

DORANTE:	But where is His Turkish Highness? We should like, as your friends, to pay our respects.
M. JOURDAIN:	I think if you look over there you will see him processing in this direction; and I've had my daughter sent for, to be formally given away. *(Enter CLÉONTE as the Turk.)*
DORIMÈNE:	Your Highness, may I kiss your hand? *(CLÉONTE offers his hand, and she kisses it.)* We are friends of your future father-in-law, and we –
M. JOURDAIN:	No, no, no, that won't get through, we need the interpreter to tell him what you're saying. Then he'll answer you. He speaks Turkish like a native. Sounds gorgeous, too. Hey! Where's that fellow gone? *(To CLÉONTE.)* Strouf, strif, strof, booli-wooli winky? – I'm not getting through am I. This gentleman is a Grande Signor, this lady is a Granda Dama – Grande Signor, Granda Dama – understand? – No. Bollocks. Look. He is a French Mamamouchi. She is a Mamamouchioness. Right? Oh, Christ, where's the translator? *(Enter COVIELLE, in disguise.)* Where have you been? We can't communicate without you. Please tell him in his own language that this lady and gentleman who are my friends are two persons of the highest quality here in France. – Wait till you hear him speak . . . !
COVIELLE:	Alabala crociam acci boram alabamen.
CLÉONTE:	Catalequi tubal ourin soter amalouchan.
M. JOURDAIN:	Isn't it magical?

COVIELLE: He said, "May the rain of plenty fall on the garden of your life forever."

M. JOURDAIN: I told you he spoke Turkish, didn't I?

DORANTE: Never heard anything like it, old boy.
(Enter LUCILLE.)

M. JOURDAIN: Come along, girl, come along, so that I can give your hand to this fine gentleman who has done you the honour of proposing to you.

LUCILE: Why on earth are you dressed up like that, Father? Are you acting in a play?

M. JOURDAIN: What would I be doing in a stupid play? I'm a real person! And this is a most material matter. I intend you to take this man for your lawful wedded husband.

LUCILE: Husband? Him?

M. JOURDAIN: Yes, husband, him! Now, give me your hand, and give thanks to heaven for your good fortune.

LUCILE: I'm not marrying that.

M. JOURDAIN: You are marrying that, I am your father and I'm telling you.

LUCILE: I shan't!

M. JOURDAIN: Oh, the incessant racket! Do as I say!

LUCILE: No, father, I will not. I have told you. I will marry no-one but Cléonte, and there is no power that can make me, and before I succumb to a – *(She recognizes CLÉONTE.)* silly, childish tantrum like this I will try and remind myself that you are my father after all and really I ought

85

to obey you unconditionally; therefore dispose of me just as you wish.

M. JOURDAIN: Good girl! I am pleased to see you remember your filial duty. Proves you were brought up nice. *(Enter MME. JOURDAIN.)*

MME. JOURDAIN: What's going on here? Eh? Rumour has it you are marrying our daughter to an itinerant magician.

M. JOURDAIN: For the last time, shut it, shitbag. I am sick to the back teeth of you meddling in my affairs. Is there no possibility of teaching you how not to be a total embarrassment?

MME. JOURDAIN: You are the embarrassment in this house. You reel from one folly to the next. Who are this shower of vagrants?

M. JOURDAIN: I intend to marry Lucile to the son of the Sultan of Turkey.

MME. JOURDAIN: The son of the Sultan of Turkey!

M. JOURDAIN: Yes, the son of the Sultan of Turkey! You can prostrate yourself to him through the interpreter here.

MME. JOURDAIN: I don't need an interpreter. I am quite capable of telling him to his face that he hasn't a chance of my daughter.

M. JOURDAIN: For the very, very last time –

DORANTE: Surely, Madame Jourdain, you cannot oppose this most profitable match? Are you implying that you would reject His Royal Turkish Highness as a son-in-law?

MME. JOURDAIN: Dear God, will you mind your own business for once?

DORIMÈNE: It's quite an honour; I wouldn't say no to it.

MME. JOURDAIN: There's not much you would say no to.

DORANTE: It is only our warm friendship with your family and yourself, Madame, that prompts us to intervene in a domestic matter. MME. JOURDAIN: I can live without friendship.

DORANTE: But look, your daughter yields to her dear father's wishes!

MME. JOURDAIN: My daughter has consented to marry a filthy Turk? She can forget poor Cléonte just like that?

DORANTE: What mightn't one do to become a great lady?

MME. JOURDAIN: I'd strangle the hussy with my own two hands if she ever thought of such a thing!

LUCILE: Mummy –

MME. JOURDAIN: Get away, strumpet.

M. JOURDAIN: Are you scolding the girl because she's been obedient?

MME. JOURDAIN: Yes! She's my blood as much as she's yours.

COVIELLE: Madame.

MME. JOURDAIN: What?

COVIELLE: A word.

MME. JOURDAIN: There are quite enough words already without you adding to them.

COVIELLE: Monsieur, get her to speak to me in private, and I think I can bring her around.

MME. JOURDAIN: Nobody's bringing me anywhere. I'm stopping here.

COVIELLE: Just listen to me.

MME. JOURDAIN: No.

M. JOURDAIN: Listen to him for God's sake!

MME. JOURDAIN: No. I'm not listening to anyone. She's not getting married. It's not negotiable. The end.

M. JOURDAIN: Oh, the colossal obstinacy of women! She's getting married because I say she's getting married, and that's all there is to it!

COVIELLE: Please listen to me for one moment. Then you can do what you like.

MME. JOURDAIN: . . . Ten seconds. That's all. Just to get shot of you. *(COVIELLE takes her aside.)*

COVIELLE: Madame, we've been winking at you since you walked in the room! Can't you see that all this is only sucking up to your husband's grand ambitions? We're all in disguise! And Cléonte himself is playing the son of the Sultan of Turkey!

MME. JOURDAIN: . . . Oh dear.

COVIELLE: Whilst making a meal of the small part of the interpreter is – Coville!

MME. JOURDAIN: Ah. I see what you're about.

COVIELLE: Act ignorant for the time being. If you can.

MME. JOURDAIN: *(Aloud.)* Well, that settles it, then; I consent to the marriage.

M. JOURDAIN: At last! Reason prevails. Why wouldn't you listen to him sooner? I knew he'd be able to tell you precisely what it will mean to have a Sultana in the family.

MME. JOURDAIN: He explained all that very well, and I'm satisfied. Send out straight away for a notary.

DORANTE: Well said! And, Madame Jourdain, in order that I may set your mind at rest concerning the nature of the relationship between your husband and the beautiful Countess, let me reassure you that you may banish every twinge of jealousy for ever, because the same notary will marry her to me.

MME. JOURDAIN: I'm satisfied with that too.

M. JOURDAIN: *(Aside to DORANTE.)* Brilliant! That'll put her off the scent.

DORANTE: *(Aside to M. JOURDAIN.)* Yes. So long as we keep up our marital charade.

M. JOURDAIN: Let's have this notary, then!

MME. JOURDAIN: Jourdain. Since everyone else if off to the altar, what about Nicole?

M. JOURDAIN: I give Nicole to the interpreter. Lucile to her Turk. And my wife to anyone who'll have her! *(They all embrace, except MME. JOURDAIN, who weeps. A wedding dance to end the play.)*

THE END